Yes You May

John Tucker

chipmunkapublishing
the mental health publisher

All rights reserved, no part of this publication may be reproduced by any means, electronic, mechanical photocopying, documentary, film or in any other format without prior written permission of the publisher.

>Published by
>Chipmunkapublishing
>United Kingdom

http://www.chipmunkapublishing.com

Copyright © John Tucker 2025

POETRY COLLECTIONS BY THIS AUTHOR FROM CHIPMUNKA

Soundcloud Rain

The Sunset Child

Breath Trapped In Heaven

Brave New Tense

VISION

"Look Fufie I can fee feep."

'Garden' is the password to my imaginary world.

There is a catflap on the radio there. Sunlight forms a golden pool on the closed eyelids of the fool as he lays out on the garden's lawn. When he opens his eyes he sees cloud-forms floating by outside but the rest of this no, not-so-special-perception is gone.

Something about being a Starvationist.

Something about Autumn as Optimus Prime.

Still there is no such thing as Time.

Autumn is a time when wasps leave fag-burns in the apples, apples with toe-nails embedded in their cores, and the air has a plaintive, melancholic, wistful, elegiac note and tone… it's when the leaves start to fall down.

Down in London we only had a postage stamp garden. I used to sit out there with my brother and observe ants on the blades of grass. I would ask myself if I too were but an ant unto some higher God.

I remember having a love of hammers.

It reminds me that my dad might call his poem 'The Grit of The Angels,' underline it with WD40, tap a nail in with a hammer and watch it spread its wings.

John Tucker

WOKEN EARLY ON A MONDAY MORNING

I've woken from a shocking dream.

I went back to Harecroft Hall -

the school I attended when small -

and looked in the woods for a game.

When the government drove me away

at the end the monster I'd seen

in that dream-kingdom of green

and clear as the light of day

had been understood the result

of nuclear testing nearby.

It left its death on the eye.

I felt the shame of the insult.

When I woke it was but the bird,

that monster, nothing more,

and still against the Hollow Claw

in spirit or was it in word.

That's why I'd gone back to check,

to hunt for my discovery,

in dreams, where we're free

as the running of the beck

but in dreams the bird became

that monster, in the wood,

and doing what they thought they should,

the government silenced my name.

The last thing before I woke,

I was driven off in their van.

For I'd seen upon my return

the monster they couldn't shake.

They didn't want it leaking out,

that there'd been a nuclear leak,

of which we could not speak,

with either sadness or doubt.

That's why the monster came

in dreams but not the bird

in wake when still unheard

the witness was not to blame.

NOTES ON HYPER-VISION IN THE YEAR 2000

I

MILLENNIAL PEN-KNIFE TOOLS

A virtual death machine to wake you up. A word-chord synthesiser at the edge of selection. A drug called "Strictly Free" that does what it says on the tin, is and makes you strictly free to consume. A red-bleeding type-writer inside a ping-pong ball. An holographic horse-cock wheeled in the bedroom. An invisible square of air called 'Mosaic by Darth Vader' stroked on telly. A neutraliser drink that sobers you up in one quick instant. The monolith from 2001: A Space Odyssey protruding from the oldest fell at ten to eight. Earphones implanted with tiny mics inside them so that you can record on them. A love-bomb that explodes in a Chaos Theatre. What's wrong with these is that they are not real!

II

MILLENNIAL PROPHECIES

I look into that dust in that late sunbeam angling in and foresee that they will one day hunt for something called the God Particle that will prove God non-extrinsic to matter.

It would be good to see an alignment of the Plough and the landscape for a first black President of America.

I think if Fight Club were real someone would fly two planes into the Twin Towers on September 11th and I don't think that a good idea but someone might do that.

I would like to write a book, maybe a Trilogy, called The Scientific Papers, classed as a series of findings into itself, into the concept of art and science as a single discussion of perception.

It would be good if there were a party in an office block where all the internal walls are removed and where every floor represents a decade in music, fashion and substances.

I myself would like to record an album on earphones, like Rimbaud might if he were a musician.

I would say that smells from tellies would also be possible one day too.

I think what we might see is an Age called the Age of Enchantment that is an echo of the Enlightenment.

I do wonder if there will be another immaculate conception now that we have a new Millennium.

III

MILLENNIAL AMBITIONS

To replace the archaic word for 'gay' would be amazeballs because 'gay' used to be Man's highest emotion and was never replaced.

To discover an aesthetic anti-system like the colours of the vowels in English would also be great, even though Rimbaud deemed it folly.

To conduct an experiment into the international language alphabet would also be an artistic ambition.

To overthrow the conscious self-censor would be good, maybe create a superhuman narrator called FUCK who can tell the truth like no-one else.

To start a new religion is what I am getting at because I think the Millennium means what is old is expended and we need to renew our values; and already Jedi is an official religion on the census forms in London.

To start a new language entirely would also be a positive thing, if at all possible, in my opinion.

I would like to start the tradition of the post-poem.

I would also see gypsy poetry in the English centre because it would shake things up and I think it could be interesting to see if they have anything new to offer.

If I were a concept artist I'd build a room made of hash that the audience can blow-torch but as I am not, just a writer, I can't do that; and I would only endorse real live death in the cinema if an old granny volunteered for euthanasia and that's because I do have some moral compass.

To make a new discovery as big as fire is the long and short of it, for every generation might have that chance again, to usurp the burning torch of culture from the old.

To bring back the Summer of Love is the largest and widest goal.

To bring about simultaneous orgasm of Man.

IV

DIRTY WORK

"You know how dad told us all

he was an art smuggler nicknamed Blue?

That he smuggled art over the Berlin Wall?

That he sold his business when

the Berlin Wall fell? Well,

I think it might've been code,

might've been recourse to euphemism.

I think he was a pollen smuggler.

I think he had a pollen farm

way up high in the Moroccan

mountains and shipped tonnes

and tonnes of pollen to the States.

This whole art dealer nicknamed

Blue thing is just to protect us.

At least this is what I entertain.

I also think he named us after

The Doors, John, James, and Robert

Yes You May

and then they had a girl of course.

Have you noticed we are born

in a season each, going Spring,

Autumn, Winter, Summer, and

march right left right left in the hands?

There are also four compass

points, four seasons, four wheels

of a car and four dimensions

to the mapping of any point in

the spacetime continuum including

time. Now revolve that bifter!

After all I think Jesus himself

would be a proto-hippy stoner

poet in this day and age. Ah,

I love it when the Wizard of Oz

resolves into colour. There are

casual drug references all around us.

Mario mushrooms confer energy.

Tinkerbell's dust makes you

fly. And in the Wizard of Oz

they lie down in the field of

poppies and see the Emerald City.

So hurry up passing that joint.

Or else we'll never stop the war."

V

WHAT IT FEELS LIKE TO BE DYING OF CANCER

A Russian has a right to a square of red perceived by someone from another land and Liberty and Trade go hand in hand.

Smell is the most primal sense, in love, absent in cinema.

Blissful Lovingness is where all religions meet.

Better and worse are but materialistic, Western concepts.

The Age of Communication momentarily endorses, means the Age of Alienation.

Each age is unable to see its own prejudices, its own cage of retrospective categorisation.

The Age of Enchantment is an echo of The Enlightenment.

The Enlightenment is the simultaneous astrological and sociological de-centering of Man.

The opposite of something is the pre-requisite.

The pre-verbal, the thought-pattern, into words, via the mechanics of meaning, is dilution.

The condition of knowledge produces no Triumph.

When you renounce the quest for meaning, you find it, fall back on meaning-by-proxy.

When you lose your concentration you die.

Your ordinary speech is surreal enough.

There are too many words in the world.

Everything living shares the same heartbeat in a given lifespan.

The artist is the missing link reintegrating into a society of worms below and the artistic spirit androgynous.

You should not trust systems for they rule with fear not love.

All guns should be flown in a spaceship into the heart of the sun.

Without difference no contradistinction.

Everyone is my brother and I love them.

The symbol [R] represents the stance that there is room for Creativity in the synapse gulf, that the creative spark is not all mappable/ predictable in advance.

There is no more mapless space.

Fear is an epiphany of Hell in the self.

Philosophy is a self-contained language corresponding to nothing real in life.

Existentialism is a child at the pick and mix with a credit card.

Politics is a choice between two plates of dogshit.

It is better to have a cup of tea than it is to kill yourself.

Portability is the new apotheosis of Form.

I. T. might stand for Instant Travel too.

All things must be returned to earth, surrendered like a rented thing to death.

John Tucker

AWAY WITH THE FAIRY LIQUID

As if even Natural things are given over once again to a Barthesian world of product placement, it might be instructive to consider the healing of my busted, dusty Hooverbag lungs... once I was away with the Fairy Liquid. I became interested in the switch thrown. There were new maps sprawled on the point of a pin. I hungered after The Snowbell Prize. My brief fling with the politics of flight kept me up all through the Ancient Night. Another high-powered dawn was born but what was the WATTAGE? Well, I felt a leaf, I fell out of life, probably no-one else knew, but then there may be some. I wallowed in my lazy swamp, languishing, lizarding, long. Interstellar Artois was the effect of fat, planetary raindrops beating down on sad, Lucozade lights, lying lambent on the paving stones. DogMuckels was not what it seemed. Quantity Streets were typical of consumer culture. By now, the National Hypochondriac Service have sorted me out. My mood is made stable on a sterilised table. Fakeazade does not come free from the kitchen Tap as yet, but we are working on it. Erase the Dettol. There's no such thing as cinnamon, but then again that is not strictly true. Well-weird this ward: words woke it: walls broke it: Weirds walk it: or they should, break it open to the light of day, straight away. There's little to do except listen to the snap, crackle and pop of the cereal, cereal in the morning after a dark night of the soul in winter.

A HAPPY KNACK WITH THINGS OF DIRT

I had a happy knack with

musical concepts back in my youth -

one was to do with Nirvana…

Sullen, silken sulks,

we drink the same rain,

spit is clean

and so is dirt.

Another was when I came into possession

of a Pearl Jam tape that was cut in the reel.

After a delicate operation

to reseal the reel it had

a small pause in the music,

so the ideal was to do away

with the small pause, by chanting

"another, another, another fucking joint."

My mnemonic for the strings became

Even A Dick Gets Big Erections.

I recorded a little album on binaural earphones,

said on the record I would

"plug my senses in the mains."

I wrote a paper about whether or not

Lucy in the soul w/ demons

happens to be an actual substance

but it got lost, maybe in the void!

My first mobile started to reverberate

the rhythm of 'William Tell'

through every technological inlet in the room

before it rang from home.

There was a call to tattoo

someone's name on

Piper At The Gates of Dawn,

Yes You May

and finally the one that takes the biscuit

is when I discovered my brother's

sheet where pictures grew.

The pictures it would seem

do depict the lyric to

a song I wrote back when

I was trying to be Kurt Cobain -

but still it wasn't mine

because I didn't lay it down.

That pretty much sums up

what I was doing with my musical youth -

and now here I sit (   ) striving

not for effect but still

struggling to just talk.

After garage and house comes library.

Voices could be quavers,

could be onjects,

could be syllabubbles,

could be sonic machinations

at the periphery of sound

and most importantly

the colours of the vowels.

They ask you to increase

your threshold of

Negative Capability.

Meanwhile there's something I think I know

and shouldn't impart

but it's because

I have a heart;

and writing a letter Dear Music

could be instructive in mental health

in the future; and putting

Paradise Lost to music

shouldn't be done

unless it's going to be amazing,

so it's an aesthetic

not moral question.

I also remember, when

Aphex Twin's new double album

came out around the Millennium,

it was comparable to Stravinsky's

The Rite of Spring.

I failed to make it an essay,

while my brother-poet Dedalus

was writing of how Autechre

is the heir to Wagner.

I look back and consider

the road of rock n roll cliché

as leading only to sadness.

It is a wanker'd planetarium of ego -

but then all of a sudden

and just like that

only songs can survive

the shipwreck of the soul -

because songs are Portable.

ENJOY YOUR FOOD

M & S Food, says the empty carrier bag

discarded on the bedroom floor -

does that mean Karl Marx

or Howard Marks?

Either way I no longer puff

the evil weed anymore

which back in the day

some Londoners labelled "food"

as if all the labels

in the cupboard swapped round...

and do the giggling stars

themselves not swap places

when no-one is looking?

O glow-in-the-dark stars on the ceiling!

How nutritious you can seem!

A shimmer, a glimmer,

a salesman's pitch!

Speaking of which,

it is pitch black outside.

No stars illuminate the garden.

The dark garden was once alive with eyes!

In here, wilted daffodils

that once signified peace,

love and happiness

in the very texture

of their yellow petals

now should be thrown out,

stoop down, instead of pout…

it must be sad to have to

stoop in funeral robes.

Yes You May

I look about me at other things

between myself and the walls -

a calender, a cork Notice Board,

a wall-chart listing the names

of the plants of the redolent meadows…

there is a dead telly wearing

mother's black, funeral hat,

and a work of art made of wood!

There is more, adorning

the room but all of it is indomitable.

Anyhow I was talking of food,

in the traditional sense;

and there is little of it

but Baked Beans on toast is good.

It shows consumer culture

even stretches this deep into the sticks,

where finding sticks for the fire

is a prominent concern…

here at this monastic retreat

I would rather feel cold

than not have enough to eat -

but others are the other way round.

Earlier I had the crumbling cheese.

Before that a bacon butty for breakfast.

Now I am quenched and sated,

but like a fast car, made

to best drive above the limit,

the lusty engine drives me on.

I think it is water I should cherish -

that I should carry and sip a pint.

Already compress sans sugar,

Yes You May

I like to be, but find I can't.

Even the Baked Beans have sugar in them.

Still, under the surfaces

hides the diary of a saint.

John Tucker

BACK AGAIN

Back again – at the honeytrap

of the flat, anti-Romantic laptop screen -

venting my spleen – but

to what purpose may I ask?

Is anything from this age going to last?

Is it all "use just once and then discard?"

I've been eating Take away pizza,

(vegetarian hot), bought

from the local Take-away joint in town.

I've been drinking Diet Coke.

At 42 the best would be done;

for peak time is over by now;

but maybe there is yet room

to incorporate the number 3484?

As if to arraign and inveigh against

the way even breath is costed

in totalitarian capitalism?

Sirens are calling from the rocks.

It's time for my evening medication.

Any glance at the clock

around this time is a reminder

like the whole business

of writing is a machine

for remembering to take my meds.

The pills are not sweeties though,

in a sugar-coated world.

They are for srs difficulties -

to placate and suppress more

than address things in talking therapy -

for the paradigm of psychoanalysis

has been replaced by neuroscience

where all illness is seen as

chemical imbalances in the brain

which some think is rather crude.

So I ingurgitate my chemical food.

Now it is later. My brother has been down

for some cereal, cereal in the night.

He polished off the Shreddies,

but left some Weetabix.

It is I that was the seer

associated with the oldest fell, but

by now meds weigh heavily down on my soul.

Nothing by means of vision

nor wild hallucination either

has passed by these senses for a while.

I mean if I detailed a list of every access

of wonder, every inscape

of wings, every visionary

proclivity, every piece of

pollen in the pollen count,

it would take ages…

instead I start to think about a rose

poking its redolent nose

and its redolent pose

through stolid concrete…

micro millimetres of birth-push

will bring it standing

before an audience of waves

even though it is only an image.

Clap for the rose,

O audience of waves,

for it could dissimulate

the mating queen

from the green

pages in the flesh...

and we could do well

to pursue her fume

into a moon-glow chamber!

TEAR-JERKING SENTIMENTAL ENDING SCENE

The friends I've made

I'd like to keep

and brush their hair when

we get to sleep

I think this illness

is a monster

chill with the stillness

and love yr brother

the severed notebook

went on for ages

with no connection

in all its severed pages

I hate these voices

these infernal voices

I made my choices

they were not James Joyce's

now I want to stay free

I want to stay me

I stay calm

in all uncertainty

and I want to stay cool

and not be the fool

who was the Smartest

kid in school

O crossroads of

all inward spiral

I hope your smile

does not go viral

the severed notebook

itches with skunkosis

in my back pocket

pre-diagnosis

and I now look back on

youth that's flown

over the houses

into the unknown

Yes You May

today it's snowing

there is no knowing

if the creative

juices are flowing

and I want to stay free

and I want to stay me

and I want to stay calm

in all uncertainty

yes I want to stay clear

as a morning beer

now that you know

I'm the ancient seer

and I live for you

GUTTERBY

Nowhere in my knowledge is it any more evident

that Nature is a great art exhibition

than down on Gutterby Beach

where I walked with my love…

there is no map to follow,

from Alex Garland's famous novel,

for a curved A to B trajectory

will take you down to Silecroft -

but you can follow the procession of natural

monuments of rock as you go:

the first is Dark Fortress Rock,

barnacle-clad and casting a shadow -

for we liked to re-name things

as we wandered in animistic trance,

and booted the bruised football,

and noted the usual, single washed up shoe,

the pebbles gleaming but dull,

the gulls circling overhead,

the driftwood smoothed by hands

of mermaids under the waves,

the way the waves make

Yes You May

gentle love to the shore…

and what scent to the air as well!

The other rocks I cannot recall

the names of, but they were not fixed

and formal, merely impromptu appellations.

If you are lost and need directions,

following the rocks is in order

but I'm sure you'll know how to navigate

the ragged beauty of the beach.

MY 'H'

Like Norman Nicholson about to enter space

I thought I'd come back on and say

I will soon be giving up on words

and take up the wordless poem, having

developed a free and unique style

of stress-relieving, acid-casualty doodles…

they are elegant at every turn of the pen,

and would seem tribal to you.

Before I do that I thought I should empty my heart,

relate something about how we are

all but iron filings firked to the moon;

how we are flying into the filament of bird;

how I see the candle not the Bunsen-burner still…

but then we'd get the problem of the pollen count unsaid.

All those things I haven't factored in like finding

perfumed moonlight in a clearing in the wood;

how I delight in the way that a bird

can fly from right to left and why too.

This time when I take the journey

away from words to the realm of distraction,

they might be letters, those doodles,

might be toy money, might be lines of law,

or anything imaginable. They might be my H;

and I will try to not come back again!

WALL IS SHIT

"Wall is shit," as she said in a dream.

Or rather when I woke, feeling

befuddled. I soon found my way

downstairs and drank a cup and

took my morning meds and got back

to the wall. She's right, it's shit.

I've got wall-cancer or had it.

Rearranging regrets in permutations,

like bricks, won't help anything.

METAMORPHOSE

I found a lump of something

under Black Combe's summit,

under the watchful gaze

of its bald, blank forehead,

but could not identify it

in name nor in function

down here at the foot

where the cars come to pass.

I left little teeth marks

imprinted in the nugget

which was not a truffle

because of its savoury flavour.

It struck me that I should

leave the incognito thing alone,

eat a mini Mars Bar instead,

and go about my business.

John Tucker

MY DIAGRAM DIAGRAM

The sheet where pictures brown and blue

simply bloomed or maybe grew

was not the work of Winnie the Pooh…

I discovered it when my father passed.

Down in the smoking den in the barn,

smoke made ancient ghost-faces in the dark.

The pictures themselves seem to depict

the lyric to a song I wrote, way back

in a teenage band called Oedipus Wrecks

but the sheet is not my sheet. I concede

it is my younger brother's, for he

is the one that laid it down. <BEE>

might well soon ensue from @

in the international language alphabet

according to him and his cutting wit.

The rest for me is but mere consolation

prizes for God's unwanted children

whom it seems are still glad to be born.

ENTRANCE

I got a First from Lancaster University in a time of difficulty created by mental illness. Last time I wrote one of these was nearly twenty years ago and I was at the time reading Proust waft into elaborate sub-clauses and privileging the language at first hand, whatever that meant in its New Beat fashion. Because it's a tried and trusted measure I can report that by now I am reading Wittgenstein. What a philosopher! In Wittgenstein I believe I have found 'my philosopher.' He says a lot of pain is caused by misunderstanding the logic of language, and hopes to remediate it with a process of elucidation. I myself believe in Will Fenn's idea that love is grouped with language not God, and so we should tend to our language-use. This is why I wish to further pursue literature on a course.

THANK YOU JARVIS

Thank you Jarvis Cocker

for the best first LSD trip

anyone could ask for.

It was taken with a prayer

at my first Glastonbury,

when Dylan was on

at smouldering sunset

and we squelched in

the good, glad mud, wearing

bin liners over our boots

and huddled together

for a heartbeat-to-heartbeat

then you guys came on stage

at Nightfall just as we came up

and it was electric, the

way you kicked in

with The Fear, the

lights, the music…

it all left you feeling

Glastonbury should be free.

Those were happy days,

writing 12 poems for Natalie

on the roof of the house

where the Plough aligns,

playing gigs in Oedipus

Wrecks, in London pubs,

not to mention

the essay in detention

about a green parrot sent

to space through the conch.

The leather jackets used to

hang round Camden Town

and once we came up

north on holiday and

attained the island of penguins!

Already love was grouped

with language not God,

already love was

a choice of words.

And where are we now?

And what happened when

we were supposed to

meet up in the year 2000?

People can change

beyond recognition fast -

a bad trip, a school too far -

then old friends are discarded -

and forever lamented too.

John Tucker

THE BEST ONE I'VE DONE SINCE I WAS A STUDENT

Your pretext extends beyond

emptying space of the human form.

I note how philosophy and *poesis*

differ on the notion of the system:

in the former we hear of the triumph

of so and so's system, but

in the latter systems are not

to be trusted for they rule

with fear not with love.

Whenever I think I'm through

with all things loving you

my mother comes in the kitchen

and starts chopping vegetables.

As if for humour, gravity and katabasis

she makes me put asparagus

in a pint glass with water

at the bottom like flowers.

Then I might insufflate

the vapid fume of my Vape;

and then I might recognise

I left out the crisp packet.

So to love's infinite, polyform permutations

I turn but have to turn away

where you love me not,

and all I haven't got, and so

no longer do I cling to the dream.

I hereby temper the wild,

Romantic, impassion'd

proclivities of my temperament,

learn the falsehood of my opinions

and journey from idealism to pragmatism.

I hereby abjure nursing

the suffering of my ideals

if only to free you in spirit

which seems a gentlemanly thing to do.

A thesis as thin as the Rizla it's in,

light it and write it, burn and unlearn,

can lead all the way to the loony bin,

make you forget how to spell

Winnie the Pooh. Or how

old you happen to be.

It was an endless sea.

I was knocked back

at a remove from

my own consciousness.

I was unable to see

the international language alphabet

because all I could see was

the international language alphabet.

It seems like hiding

from *The Waste Land*

inside *The Waste Land*…

and what a refreshing change it makes

to not be manufacturing fakes

in the land of flying fairy cakes.

YOU WERE COMING HOME

(for baby Florence)

I was walking through the clouds,

with a song against my ear,

and when I made it through the crowds,

there was reason enough to cheer,

'cause you were coming home,

yeah you were coming home,

and I just want say "hey! Go with the flo'!"

for you are such a beautiful one,

as beautiful as the English sun,

which so often tries to hide,

and we love you deep inside.

You're coming with your mum and dad,

protected by a red guitar,

and though you're uncle has gone mad,

you're still going to be a star,

'cause you are coming home,

yeah you are coming home,

Yes You May

and I just want to say "hey! Go with the flo'!"

for you are such a beautiful one,

as beautiful as the English sun,

which so often tries to hide,

and we love you deep inside.

John Tucker

SONG FOR LITTLE BABY FLORENCE

It's funny writing for you before we have met

but I'm the uncle that taught your mum the alphabet

now she types much faster than I ever could do

and she's gifted the world with a beauty like you

it's a celebration just to have you around

it's a time for listening to The Velvet Underground

it's a time for breaking into spontaneous song

welcome to the family which is where you belong

soon you'll be walking and will make them proud

like I was once walking up on a cloud

and you'll know the meaning of the verb to love

like I know it too with my excellent bruv

it's a day of happiness to first have you here

it's a day for cheering and for drinking beer

it's a day for playing with the toys on the floor

and for going with the flow as before

MOTLEY FRIDGE MAGNET LETTERS

What a strange man,

whom it seems

comes in the kitchen

and asseverates

that "the face of stars

was scripted by Jesus"

and then launches

into a braggart monologue about

whatever else he got up to

in an extraordinary life

before he even left school,

until his mum puts

a stop to his boasting.

What must it be like

to hear someone

determine something like that,

and more to the point

what must it be like

to have not attained

the face of stars?

It doesn't make

the others feel like playing,

that the strange man in question

had obtained the vision,

a cosmicomic smile

on a round face with two eyes.

VORTEX

A tear-jerking violin

in a rainy rugby match

wants to be Arthur Rimbaud

but cannot make the transaction

for all that it dreams

that the heartbeats are stars.

Cigarettes hold it back

from running too freely

as you may well know

and even homemade LSD

that makes movement leave traces

like the pollution of cars.

Its sunset comes in upturned jars.

It has been with the ocean.

It has been with the shapeshifter.

It has been with Nintendo.

And it knows that science

would soon have little to counter,

and it knows that imagination

doesn't make it unreal,

and it knows of the vortex

where its song resonates.

It knows.

HURRAY

After Flora comes gay

in the international language alphabet.

After acid comes *Bic*

and acid is a bet with the mind,

the marriage of Alice and Pan,

a spirit-level for the spirit -

but after Flora comes gay.

It might be why I am so bored,

sitting here typing away

at the foot of the oldest fell,

skint, single, mentally ill,

medicated, car-less, unemployed, living

with my mother still in the sticks,

no neighbourhood, no amenities,

a pretty place nevertheless.

There doesn't seem a place for me

in the overall Social Order,

except sitting in the kitchen, venting

my spleen at a laptop screen, supping

drinks like I were a chinwagging

tea-hag of Time like my dad.

My best work was all

about the 25th of May,

which is my sister's birthday.

I contemplate the four collections

I still have out with *Chipmunka*

and am not too displeased,

though when they say

I should redo the now-retracted

Rose Petals In The Ashtray

I know it's now too late.

I took an O. D. the likes of which

it was genius to survive

but coming back down

from the chemical equation of it all

I lost the ability to ejaculate.

Now the local lasses say

if I've not got the juice for them

then I am gay, and so

I think I am, but it might be

that I am cut off from the verb,

the doing word, that is love.

I have had a gay experience

or two before, but walked away,

wishing I were with a woman.

O WHERE IS THE NET?

O where is the net,

pussy willow that smiled on this leaf?

Is it in the trees

and in the breeze?

At seven I wrote a text, encrypting

a sophisticated node to do with Gravity, storing

the idea of the net in writing

in the attic to give it a chance to grow

all the way round the world, also conducting

an experiment into the maths

of the new colour as a cellular mark, and separating

the object "pollen" from its name.

This was before the world wide web;

and the cloud is mentioned

before the net in the book!

The net already existed

in the American military,

but the net is ancient…

it appears in Lowell, as it

appears in James Joyce as a prophecy.

I even heard Shakespeare

had a son called Hamnet.

Yes I would say it is blowing in the breeze,

but also exists as a stack in California.

That's where they eat acid-tabs

and come out with microchips.

THE ABSOLUTION OF HANNAH

My sister has been the only one

that knows I am a G.

She has known I am a G

since we lived on Lynton Road

and I played her a song and showed

her a Smashing Pumpkins tape.

I was the one that smuggled her

in my bed at night when we were young,

to play I Spy in the fecund dark,

spider spider on your back

which finger did that. Now

she has a little baby girl of her own.

She had to keep trying

as I do too when it comes to my work.

Yes You May

I imagine nothing could be more

exciting than her keeping trying

and nothing more boring

than me with my work.

Even when she was born

she was a little ray of light,

deft left hand born of another

deft left hand, meaning my mum.

WINDOW

I look out the window – two cars,

contiguous or co-extensive to each other.

Also the yew tree guarding the gate.

Above it the sky is unblemished blue.

The window is a narrow one too.

Leaves of Virginia creeper

have crowded its edges. I

also see how overgrown

Everything has become, the drive,

the ivy hedge, the flower-bed, the lane.

If my father's passing galvanised us

to do up the house and build a patio,

we soon enough let the garden

go to seed in his sore absence.

The levels of green have gone obscene.

In fact the garden has got gangrene.

Through this defamiliarisation

of perception, this ostranenie,

I look out and note how the wind

wags the leaves like dog tongues,

and sways the trees, like the tree's boughs

Yes You May

are playing basketball or stroking a cat.

I hear music leak in from

another room where once I sat.

John Tucker

POEM

Because I am not after you anymore

because   I   am   not   after   you
because I am not

I dare to take strength,

take courage from the rain

it isn't even raining though

but a warm summer night

where I have taken my medication

and sup on artificially sweetened instant

coffee, free of clock-time

I am no sad king

alone with his kingdom

only poor old John

my skis dangle from trees

when I hear the ego-loss breeze

and Google my senses

in the garden that is gone

I picture buried treasure

on the end of a line of string

it tautens and tightens

to a chain of music from star to star

John Tucker

WEIRD SEMEN

Semen spills like silver water,

under the bridge with the angel's daughter,

splashing with laugher in a moon-glow chamber,

turning your lover into a mother,

knowing that love is the answer,

not quite sure of its favourite author,

dreaming of things like a cure for cancer,

meaning to see through the surface of the mirror,

loving the weather now it's summer,

wishing the song of its moment is over,

into the filament of bird forever,

travelling as fast as it can and faster,

feasting its eyes on the river,

needing not to borrow a fiver,

scurrying not in a state of fever,

nor currying favour to get with Flora,

Batman and Robin over its shoulder,

desirous of her slenderest whisper,

thinking of renouncing religious fervour,

feeling like it is a slave no longer.

John Tucker

THE GENIACK

He helped invent the net at seven,

with parts of government that are hidden,

when the idea of the internet

needed storing in writing

in the attic of radio static at the foot of the fell.

By eight he was the witness

from *The Lords And The New Creatures* twice

which some say was his dad's business,

and he stayed quiet as a mouse.

By eleven he was marked

on the hand by his own experiment

into the maths of the new colour

as a cellular mark, though

it didn't turn out to be the new colour in the end.

By fifteen he had attained

the face of stars, as one of three

gathered in the shame, a vision

scripted in the Bible perhaps.

Yes You May

By eighteen he had spoken against
September 11th in the year 2000,
also written the highest-marked
English literature A-level exam
essay in the nation at 100%.

After school he recorded
an album on binaural earphones.

He had an effervescent mobile, reverberating
the rhythm of 'William Tell'
through every technological
inlet in the room before it rang.

He hosted the Plough alignment
for a rhythm change in the White House,
got a First despite mental illness,
had his name tattooed
on *Piper At The Gates of Dawn*,
worked the numinous,
purple-bleeding screen,
built the Tower of magic books

as an instrument of philosophy,

conducted an experiment into a tape

with a pause where resealed in the reel,

and upon the loss of his father,

discovered the sheet

where pictures grew.

Then he falsified the Nirvana barcode in writing

and attained visual radio, broadcasting dreams.

I would say they have given

Nobel Prizes for less; but

the man in question never earned 1p.

He looks back at the list

that covers one page

as if it is enough to retire on.

He asks himself what he has ever provided

for the species in terms of writing.

Despite being 1000's of files

deep into a virtual Brainforest,

an inchoate morass, a teeming data-tree,

Yes You May

despite having many self-publications

and amateur albums

at the last count out there,

he hasn't managed to get it down.

But he has offered some good things -

it is not true that it has been

all life and no writing.

Even if it had just been

his seven year old paper,

where the idea of the net was stored,

he should've deemed it a win.

The text in question contained the line

"I have a scar+ that is red and black."

He used a + sign for the 'f'

and then counted up, using

times, dates, inches, numbers, ages and more.

NOTE ON METHOD

Monopolising indigenous wisdom

in regimented metres is not for us.

Old-fashioned, out-moded writing likewise.

I like a poem to have something

behind the words and if not

to at least be New Beat, instant, easy,

the language at first hand.

Poems should come from within

or if collaborations then a source

you know and trust not forced

upon you by distant voices.

You shouldn't try and dictate

truth nor what your children wear,

nor how they wear their hair.

They are only young once

and we should forgive them.

We should let them play and ourselves

attain the state of Homo-Ludens too.

And I've said it before but

my brother's faded blue E-comedown

T-shirt from the year 2002

is preferable to monopolising

indigenous wisdom in regimented metres.

John Tucker

THE VIBE

The singer's the self-avowed

"peacock with the brightest feathers,"

the sound variegated in texture,

the soundwaves almost 4D

and all about it seems beautiful

like Piper would to our fathers

and the words are sweet as getting

head from Clemence Poesy...

> I like to float on the artifice of organic emotions
>
> through synthetic sounds.

> Voices, voices everywhere
>
> and yet not a drop to think!

> When one says I should write of
>
> Candyblasta – my mate's band -

                    Yes You May

              another says to keep it digital

              and only posit an hyperlink!

                                    The prevailing emotion I knew

                                    when first listening was terror

                                    and yet terror was concurrent

                                        to a magnetic attraction

                                    that drew me in until it seemed I

                                    couldn't get past 'Thunder'

                                    without feeling like my head

                                    was literally being kicked in.

So I stopped - though I thought it

an excellent album until it came

to effect my mental health

with an earth quake in my head…

the digital pulse was racy,

the waves compressed, the game

won over our band who

chose to just smoke weed instead…

                        I would say you don't get to win

                        Battle of the Bands and get

                        a First Class honours degree

                        from a top 10 University

                        at once and I elected the latter

                        and that I do not Regret

                        for all the laser lights that

                        flicker in the old Regret Industry.

          So Fry says it is penetration.

          Penetration of the is-ness of life.

          It punctures you in the soul

          to hear such scaring and emotive stuff.

Yes You May

It went through the walls and

I through it like a heated knife.

It contains computer game inflections.

It seems unreal as drinking Duff…

For spiritual reasons I think

'Black Cloud' is the best one and

my second favourite would

have to be 'Fell From A Ladder.'

I still can't imagine the

dynamic of being in the band

and how these sounds are now made

at keyboard, computer and compressor

and so I might stick it back on

and see if I can't finish the hits

and see if the earth quake

has subsided enough to endure

John Tucker

      the meaning with-held,
      the loving of ourselves to bits.

      The way art is salvation.
      The way they know it the cure.

Ah yes, that's right I love
that delight in a wilful opacity,

the wide-eyed wonder, the
Romance and the questing wire,

the music moving in time
but finding it moves in Eternity,

the backward glance at our being
in Germany sitting round a fire.

      The Romancing of the soul
        under far-fetched fading stars

Yes You May

has not died even though words

have put tired costumes on

and I still hear the same old band

even though there are no guitars

and under Gondwanaland

all the pollen has now gone

                and under the green hill

                has gone the ecstasy pill

                and we're hiding from the

                terror inside the terror as well

                and sadness gene is smitten

                with dreaming gland still

                and that's just what but

                TS Eliot at a Speak N Spell…

I think of some kind of heart-

valve mutation gleaned

from the graves of intelligence

at the gates of a dusky dawn

where wave forms terminate

and no intellectual property is owned

and how I sometimes curse

my mother for my being born.

My quest for meaning still

goes on and in music we

find meaning is faces in fire

or Hamlet's three creatures in cloud

in other words it's solipsistic

and we're insane to be

so frightened to touch it,

when it is so scaring and loud....

it would sit on my mantelpiece

Yes You May

if it were a painting, above

the fire that dances and entrances
with its hundred myriad tongues

and in the end the X we seek,
the enigmatic 'it' is love

and now we ground our dreams
in the soulfulness of songs.

Often we sat in rooms
with slick BPM's sliding down walls

and so often I felt then
a loner in the corner of the disco

and Tetris pieces falling up
in my New Beat notebook or Paul's

wishing I could sing and dance
in a morning scene, al fresco…

John Tucker

now the switch is thrown
and it would be invidious for me

to moan that someone's mum
was used in the Plough alignment

and now although in tone
I grow a bit more accusatory

it is not for the friends I remember
from this seat of containment.

It seems too mean to say
"I'd prefer someone moving rocks

in a river to change its pitch,"
so to the holistic reading I turn

not wishing to be too reductive,
when books can change and locks,

and gone is the old ethos to
light it and write it burn and unlearn…

Yes You May

the old armour would come off,
we would with laughter renew our pact,

peels of it, and become again
as if chinwagging tea hags of Time

of which of course there's no such thing
when held by music to be intact,

and in the Other Room the songs
still seem to rhyme and chime,

chime like bells, reverberating
up in the fells and strike a warm,

psychic chord, like The Lords
And The New Creatures with me

whom it seems is not an errand boy
but hears a voice looking for a form

and finds the apotheosis of

form to be Portability.

You say it's dull, poetry, and
to be fair it is, the routine,

but to this alchemy of perception,
I am bound, to this experiment,

for poetry seems to be more enduring
than music even if medication

now dulls the blind white light
of vision towards which seeing is sent…

at least now our scene has found
a literary voice that's not gone wrong,

wrong as making bleed a woman
at the age of sixty four,

which hardly seems a visionary
thing to do with one's song,

Yes You May

and doesn't seem possible, while my

blind white light is a door.

        I'd dance in a sensuous graffiti

        of blind white light in the basement

        of the party in the office block

        where every floor represents a decade

        in music, drugs and fashion in

        days of self-debasement,

        if Candyblasta came on, but

        I just can't go, so I'm annoyed.

                I remember when Night got burned

                and we listened to Aphex Twin

                and Mark said no, we must listen

                to Nick Drake instead

                because he could not tell if

                the vocal in Come To Daddy was a demon

                    which I assume means he does not

                        know if it's real or in his head.

    To go on to make dance

  music is brave and beautiful too

      and it's mellow and pleasant

      not digital punk, not an affront,

          and I also remember when

          it was written in blue

        "John is a living art installation"

        in the year 2000 on the front

of my New Beat notebook

as if I have grown opaque

and a delicate operation it has been

to make me come aware of this bummer

but I wouldn't really mind, as long

Yes You May

as I can still eat birthday cake

without leaving me feeling

the rusty metal saw of anger…

      "there is no virtue beyond fashion,"

        is one of the frontman's lines

      and I myself also wondered

      if it was not the same for vice

      and the Tourists flock to an acid

      casualty terrain full of mines

      deep in the earth in the middle

      of sleep but it isn't nice.

            That day I stood on the chair

            in the abandoned Primary School

              and announced to their band

              who were there that I was gay

I regret and retract and was

only trying to play the fool

to liberate myself through shame

as one among us would say...

we ransacked the tumulus of

postmodern selfhood for treasure,

Tetris pieces falling upwards

on the page to ecstasy,

always falling into line with

a quest for sensual pleasure

to make our visit to the Brain

Jewel Centre exquisite with mystery…

the point so far is that I still

put the music back on;

Yes You May

it waved away with freakish

intensity and seemed very rich;

and it is but a Mario mushroom

I am on and it's not gone;

and the songwriting tradition

all of a sudden eloped with glitch

        whom it would seem was dreaming

        of doom drone or whatever

        and post-punk too was in

        love with emotional hardcore

        and indie dressed as Robin

        Hood fixing its cap with a feather

        and Candyblasta took to the stage

        so mum took to the dancefloor.

She shook her bits to the hits

and other mothers did too

even though some sounds

were a bit busy for them

and the processed beat

went for a day trip to the zoo

where in a cage was found

the very godfather of Grime.

He's grown quite hairy now

and too long in the tooth

to make is as a musician

so he's sticking to the written word

and he wants not to shock you

but to shock with truth,

        maybe of the musical kind that

        with the mind's ear is heard.

We like the ring of timeless

familiarity to our tunes

like the lyric of Lucky

from OK Computer by Radiohead

and think that planes are

long since the shoes of clowns

and love our friends to bits

and are better off than dead.

        So I hope to popularise the rival

        band from back in the day

        even if it's only a few hits

        to their Soundcloud page

and champion the underdog

like John Peel in a way

because I think Candyblasta

are one of the best bands of the age.

What age it is I do not quite

know but it is a Digital one

to which I find adapting

hard despite the net

existing in my seven

year old flights of imagination

before it was invented, which

is published don't forget….

So the sound is now turned off,

it's later and a day of snow…

Yes You May

        the music exists in memory

        where it warms me like a fire,

        leaves the mind – that temple -

        feeling somewhat aglow -

        and so I feel that this must

        not become a spent flyer…

if in Nature there's no noise

only sound, and only the machine

can make noise, I'd say

it is then counter-intuitive

that the electronic music

I hear in Candyblasta's scene

is mellow and soulful sound

and I don't know what else to give.

If there's only loss of self

and recollection of self after,

there's still life and writing,

there's experience and data,

there's escape and return,

and so now it is with laughter

that I look back at Cambridge

and wonder what of later …

                        to stop the war's a good cause,

                            to cure cancer another one,

                        to help out the next witness,

                        although the game may have seen its end,

                        and although it's small, although it is

                              only us lot having fun,

which we would in time past,

I can also promote an old friend.

And what was love back then?

Handbags and waterpistols at dawn?

We saw the advent of phones,

e-mail addresses and more,

saw the Towers come down,

felt the need to mourn,

but still came up with melodies

as if they broke the law.

Melody was embarrassing then

according to Thom Yorke at least…

this could be time to quote

some words I like from the band -

John Tucker

"went for a walk in the West,

started to yearn for the East"

as if there is more creativity

on the go with the left hand!

                        Truth be told I doubt I will

                        see either my band or theirs

                        ever again but still write

                        as asked to by a little voice

                        who visited me at the foot

                        of the fell in graceful airs

                        and asked me elongate his

                        freedom as if I had a choice…

                                          a band is a good thing

                                          though Lockdown was a band too -

Yes You May

I've been in many, probably

too many, but it's not about me,

it is about them, who

would blow you away, but who

are also like a trapped

sparrow which I need to free.

In international language

and in new religion but

not that "new" exactly,

we put our faith and I

hitch-hiked on the wave

like I were truly New Beat

and now your stuff's all online

you'll surely never die…

John Tucker

if there are still too many

songwriters in the world, writing

too many songs too often

I'd rather Mark than me

writing songs but then

again to do the lighting

would be fun and it seems

I have been chosen for the poetry!

        To destigmatise mental illness

        would be another good cause

        and when they were up they were up

        and when they were down they were down

        and the waves of the sea

        went round and round of course

Yes You May

and I went on the road in England

when I went down to town

                    on the day of A-level results

                    and went busking with Paul

                    and that's where Mark found us

                    whom I can address as "you"

                    and that was when lofty

                    empires started to fall

                    and now I'm harking back

                    I'm starting to feel blue

but you were the one who taught

    detunings as much as E

    and the same crumbling of

    moral values is in each

John Tucker

        but I am not complaining

        for it was plain to see

        whatever was happening then

        it was like we had found The Beach

and no, there is no secret

chord H, it's a metaphor

for some experiential pleasure

that lies unknown and beyond

and I still believe in music

in a room with no door

as much as the pulchritudinous

and platinum blonde

        and when I was kicked out

        of Paul's house by his mum

Yes You May

    and lived on your floor

    and other floors as well

    the most Rimbaudian days

    of adventure had come

    and so I must ask myself

    of my own Season in Hell…

              I loved the days we shared,

              the levels we found with guitar

              which meant all were equal

              and all are equal still

              and I think of all my friends

              when under the evening star

              and look up and see something

              like a little Nirvana pill.

John Tucker

O liiiiiiiiiiiiiittle, bitter pill,

I still pray, which now art

in Heaven, give us this day

our come down at dawn,

when the world re-wakes palely,

which happens in the human heart,

give us peace, love and

beautiful music too - amen.

It's what the world needs right now,

peace, love and music for sure,

being as it is thrown into chaos

and Hell-fire without excuse

by which I mean I am asking

kindly to please stop the war

or else I'll never get over the

chemical sadness or cosmic blues…

>
> but who do I ask, surely not
>
> the other band whom

> my mother seems to support more
>
> than me in Battle of the Bands?

> I suppose anyone who visits
>
> the mirror here in this room

> near the beach where there is
>
> room to roam on golden sands….

>> I hope to show that life
>>
>> is one under the sun and there

>> is only one love, to be fair
>>
>> to the friends I gather on this raft,

>> whom it seems can visit the

John Tucker

        foot of the fell in sentient air -

        even when their love life

        and wife has made them daft...

the data-tree I collect has 1000's

   of semi-recursive files,

     and yet what efficacy can

     be more brave than this,

     which is to gather up my

     room full of reflected smiles,

     and remember that the breeze

     still contains a dissolved kiss,

and the sea isn't green said Syd

and I love the queen, he said,

and what exactly is a dream,

and what exactly is a joke,

Yes You May

and I happen to believe the lyrics

which he wrote were rather good,

and it is not impossible, you

see, to mend a broken yolk

      and the food is cooking in the AGA,

      and the Night has come again,

      and the war can unsettle you,

      leak in the head from afar,

      and the friends I kept are still

      sacred connections on memory lane

      and if the alphabet is a suicide note

      the Dude has lost his car,

            and when I hear the sound of

            Mark's new band I lose

            the cosmic blues I had and ponder

            what lies behind the song,

John Tucker

           and the bruise that swells,

           often nonplussing the queues

        is assuaged and all you had was righteous

           when I hoped you'd be wrong,

    but hearing the rigmarole and bling

    of this brief fling with the old

        politics of flight, I try and

        travel by predictive text,

    and most of the stories from the

    band days in Cambridge are untold,

        and most of the Hoovers still

        leave us feeling very vexed

and rock n roll's not dead yet

but dad's generation already did

what we learned to do as well,

Yes You May

and ladder'd tights are a form,

and so it's good that Mark
didn't just emulate Syd,

and the grimy, Nirvana blue light
sabre ink of guitar is warm,

      and music is only music, not
      brain surgery, not a scientific breakthrough,

      but still it keeps me awake
      at night reorganising saturnine stairs

      and it can make you feel emotion,
      can make you shed a tear too,

      send shivers down your spine,
      make stand tiny, baby hairs,

            and the lion from the heart
            of Poem Records has packed in

John Tucker

       twanging the guitar in endless
       fretboard masturbation again

       and the brain is not a computer
       for it can selfheal, and the sin

       of consciousness is not really a sin,
       when we stand in rain, in pain

and I don't think, knowing
Mark he'll know what a Zionist is,

    but he knows how to sing
    and to reach me and my mum

    likes his voice, and jests
    that it's unclear as light sabre fizz

    who should win Battle of the Bands
    and chew bisexual chewing gum.

A move towards a common currency
is made with immediate effect,

and music is leading the way,

a way we can feel the same,

and in a way your art will suffer

if all you do is get wrecked,

and Morrison says when play

dies, then it becomes the Game!

        You can't rip up a computer but

        you can tear and share bread like

        we did when food was scarce and

        method mad and music moved

        in time but belonged in infinity,

        where the Jedi keeps a solar spike,

        and so what's lost is regained,

        and life is one, and love is proved.

                My friends from London whom

John Tucker

        I took to the face of stars,

        and went on adventures with
        don't care who sings the best,

        as long as we stop the war, for
        it was not just new creatures,

        the efficacy of Jim Morrison,
        but peace as a manner'd request.

While here at the foot of the fell,
    I hear the shower going

    like the engine of a ferry,
    I also stop shovelling food,

    for I am full and so shall not
    be too greedy, knowing

    that modesty is graceful, and
    that graceful is usually good.

Yes You May

My love won't speak in nonsense

or Shakespeare or prose -

to me it is but silence through

which you can easily hear

the birds of dawn start talking

before the sunlight shows

the world stream in, so beautiful,

but I shall not shed a tear.

        When we went to Berlin, one of us

        was Beavis and one Butthead

        and that may be why we tied

        the knot of rugger-borealis,

        not just any old knot in a

        random piece of driftwood,

        and I seem to recall it was you, M,

        who that evening played Beavis….

John Tucker

      We chinked our drinks and challenged
          the dawn or rather Night,

      and changed our strides, our
      outlooks, pouting for the giant camera

          that floats on high o'er
      our heads with a flash of light,

          and we frightened the skies
          and just got closer and closer.

Now the dog is by my side,
and like snow to a petticoat earth

I surrender to the present tense,
  rinsed by cleansing flame,

  yes like snow, not surrender
  like a rented thing to death,

and try to not cheat myself out

Yes You May

of winnings in this little game -

I think I really love you, guys,
and you'll know who I mean,

whether it is my band or yours,
clingers on or the centre stage

and I risk my self esteem to say
that, miss our happening scene,

and have not much to show from
it but the rest of the fire-wage.

My mother drinks another drop
of gin in the room next door,

drops the telly remote
and I hear it with a thud,

think of how I don't even smoke
cigarettes now, not anymore,

John Tucker

let alone the previous obsession

I had with genetically modified bud.

We shouldn't be lounging

round paying no lecky or rent,

self-indulgent artists

licensing our long lethargy,

like I did back in the day

before voices came Heavensent,

like voices do now which seem

proleptic in a way to me

and by now my mood is

made stable on a sterilised table

and all I can do is vent my

spleen at a slinky laptop screen

and all of a sudden Cain pulled

out a gun and killed Abel

Yes You May

        and now that is a story even
        if it be a fictitious one

and nothing became of my music
because I walked off to get a degree

and bad things started to happen
when I made that move then

but fuck the curse that I was placed under
for hey this is not about me

it's about the other band who
came together out in Berlin

        and how the architecture was
        mournful in corners and mongrelised

        and how the beer was cheap
        and how the autumn changed our moods

        from glad to sadness and how the

John Tucker

public transport epitomised

the efficient functioning of the

heartbeat of the city, and how the dudes

           in the other band and I walked round

           drinking and without sleep

           and how the rhythms of feet

           on foreign pavements were noted down

           and how we slept in cars

           and fathomed the endless deep

           and how I was yet to discover

           the verse of Michael Hofmann…

and what a Germanic sound you

guys have gained now, like Kraftwerk,

made for the Digital Age where

it could pass through the soles of your shoes,

Yes You May

and get you dancing, in the

corner of the club where druggies lurk,

and then look at the evaporation

of your famous cosmic blues,

and the songs you write are great,

and I miss the age of the CD,

but can borrow a rhyme from Simon

of Autechre and Black And Decker

and down in Devon they say

keep music live, local and free

and by now I feel I already sound

like a grumpy old fecker

and some say music should be

all around us all the time

others that those whom

the Gods wish to drive mad

John Tucker

are sent music In their heads
be it Classical or grime

and I think we are one dreamer,
and our dream not just a fad,

and when the tumulus of postmodern
selfhood, the burial mound

is unpacked and some things are
not mine and some not yours

I hope we all look back and cherish
the breaking of ground

and remember the days I slept
for a year on student floors!

I am an algorithm of a selfhood,
an ontological excavation and

Yes You May

an existential detective case

peeling back layers of falsity

to reveal nothing underneath,

and I started as all one band

at a smouldering plasma screen sunset

in Cambridge's elegant city

and I felt a fine mesh net so finemesh

it was but static grey smoke

and fleck neither retaining

nor permitting anything at all

and I fart out of the wrong orifice

for a moment and a joke

and I hope pills were God Simulations

and did not make you feel small

for I am ohms and I am waves

and I'm underwriting the name

of the nation, and I am bigger
than what I myself comprehend

and some might say that in Keats
Autumn is already Optimus Prime

and soon this winter women's
work will come to an end.

My business is to show comity
between the other band and mine

and thus that life is one, to
reconcile a polar attraction,

to elide antagonistic elements
with music, to find a wine-

slick in a dream-meet experiment
that's gone straight to Heaven.

We used to drive down motorways

Yes You May

in two cars, each one giving

the other wanker signs as we

overtook in the long game,

and sleep was for the weak

and the big liquid dream was for living

and life was green and life was

clean inside the purgatorial flame.

Now we moan about ageing,

and not seeing each other anymore,

and reach each other still through

telepathy, psychic powers,

and the car's done some miles

and I'm sadder than before,

and on the floor of the wood

you might find gilly flowers.

John Tucker

They glow and radiate,
they smell like her perfume,

they dissimulate and denote
the transience of what we love

for beauty can be transient,
even here in this room,

where I hear the fridge drone
and the electric light's above.

Meanwhile, I am so glad
some of us attained our dreams,

and it's not the case
John Barnes is the only one,

and all the things I have to say
are embedded deeper than memes,

and what was it all about but
corrupting taste, having fun?

Yes You May

An hyperlink to Heaven, that
is my latest ambition, that my

latest invention, far better
than Facetube, that neologism,

whom it seems is already
marked, which is why I sigh,

here as I traverse the hypothalamus,
like a dark, dark chasm.

My Facetube was marked by an
experiment into the maths of

the new colour when I was a kid,
which is why I am too

ashamed to get it out, why
I live without enough love,

and hope the same thing

will never happen to you.

>This is private information,
>and fat chords ring in my ears,

>sounds come cluttering up
>into the labyrinthine conduit

>of the inner ear, as I write and
>quest after free beers,

>on this seat which is not
>such a bad place to have to sit.

NOTE ON OEDIPUS WRECKS

My friend Dr. Calculator Ptom named the teenage rock band upon hearing my songs. He used to say gnomic things like "the universe is a projection of the mind." "The G note is green on the guitar fretboard." "Born Slippy is evidence dance can have a soul." "Poetry is untranslatable because of the music." "Death is God." "Early Oasis is good for bittersweet, comedown energy." We boarded a train not knowing where it was headed in the middle of the Night in London. By now he is Dr. Calculator Thomas and the song is 'Born Slippery.'

John Tucker

THE OEDIPUS WRECKS GIG, CAMDEN TOWN, CIRCA 1998

I

SECRETS IN THE MUD

This is the sound of getting totally fucked.

Of when you first get your notebook sucked.

Of changing gold into Glastonbury mud.

Of lying down in a field with your bud.

This is the music through whom we aspire.

This is the rule book that is thrown on the fire.

This is the jam where the trousers are down.

This is the wine-shop on the edge of town.

Chorus: Glastonbury, you should be free, and all you have in your big city,

you hit my G, you make me see how I want to see,

lights go down, lights come on,

and all my sadness seems to be gone,

although I still love to be what I dream I am.

[guitar solo]

II

OCEANS SMILE

Oceans smile with liquid eyes

and fill themselves with rain.

The tide goes out and leaves me

lost, the last thing a glass gene.

Follow me to the resurrection

while the blind get crucified.

My weapon's only loaded in my eyes.

Death will come on silky wings

but I for one will not go.

A soul is endless, oceans open

and keeeeeeeps a perfect O.

Follow me to the resurrection

while the blind get crucified.

My weapon's only loaded in my eyes.

Go drink the ocean with your tea

cup, give your heart far out.

If oceans smile with liquid eyes

then they'll give you a shout.

Follow me to the resurrection

while the blind get crucified.

My weapon's only loaded in my eyes.

Too drunkenly I sail the water

on Rimbaud's smoking boat.

With whiskygills primed in fire

I sail the waves to Boot.

Follow me to the resurrection

while the blind get crucified.

My weapon's only loaded in my eyes.

(reconstructed via the new, synchronised word)

III

KILL

My eyes sting,

my teeth are bleeding raw,

too much thought

to make me sick.

Stinky clothes

and mouth become

my skin and all

these fruits I want to kill.

Give my hope,

surrender to the tide,

you can take

my remains;

but I must go,

to wash the poison

from my eyes,

before, before, before I kill.

IV

SNAKE SNAKE BUTTERFLY

Snake snake butterfly, lay me dead & close my eyes.

Angel serpentine, she waits on the Other Side.

Give me your alibi; give me chains to stop me fly;

give me night to soothe my blinded eyes:

so I can see the secrets of the skies.

We must rise, freedom falling from our eyes,

unlock doors, it's a perfect time to die,

and it's okay 'cause baby we'll go insane

but don't reach out too far for the flame.

Snake snake butterfly, lead me to the Other Side.

Angel serpentine, she waits on the Other Side.

V

VITAL SIGNS

Smile like a smile just to smile,

cast to Heaven for a while...

let's rip holes in the boat,

throw the captain overboard,

throw the angels off the bridge,

death comes and stops me getting

bored of life's soul-machine.

What we need is energy,

show me all your vital signs,

what we steal is what we need,

what we need to feel alive,

for I'm alive with vital signs.

Back to Hell to plunder wings,

let the ritual now begin,

Yes You May

come and ride the waiting beast,

ride it gone into the fire,

ride it to the waiting feast,

my baby's waiting to get higher,

to get higher, to get higher...

what we need is energy,

show me all your vital signs,

what we steal is what we need,

what we need to feel alive,

for I'm alive with vital signs,

yeah feel alive with vital signs.

Come again there's much to do,

don't you know that I love you?

VI

HEAVEN KNOWS

Heaven knows and walks away -
but what it knows it will not say.

It's impossible to make a cowboy film in space?
Heaven knows and turns its face!

Heaven's filled with silver eyes.
Heaven's hills all harmonise.

I hear its angels when they call...
Heaven knows and lets them fall!

[reconstructed]

VII

MURDER IS DEAD

Fuck this, fuck that, fuck me yeah,

I wish that I had been there,

been there to saaaaaave Jesus,

I'm sure he meant to please us.

Murder is dead,

murder is dead,

murder is dead.

We're young and filled with semen,

we're going to break some hymen,

we'll make the cops turn in their badges,

we're going over all the edges yeah.

Murder is dead,

murder is dead,

murder is dead.

VIII

THE GHOSTS LAMENT (THE GUZZLER MEN)

I'm the only one left, left to shoot my

own gun. This is the dead land. Crack a smile

and curse the sun. Death awaits to fuck me.

Give me bliss and give me kisses. Death a-

waits to save me. The ghosts lament, the ghosts

lament. Come on baaaaaaaaaby, you know it's e-

asy, don't say maaaaaaaaaybe, let's go crazy. Death

awaits to fuck me. Give me bliss and give

me kisses. Death awaits the same me. The

ghosts lament, the ghosts lament, no more ghosts.

||||.

[Note: when years later I discovered the James P D Tucker sheet where pictures grew, and the pictures seemed to depict the lyric to one of my old songs, this is the song.]

TRASH COMPACTOR MEMORY

Factory work is noble slavery.

Human error saves your life. It could be

a manufactured wing-shop. We spend our

nights in the stentorian guts of a

monster with a firehose, and cycle

home at fire-streaked dawn. Money is but pa-

per and metal. Water is but liquid

crystal juice. I'm also interested in

God Simulations. You have to stand a-

lone in Nothingness and dictate the pa-

rameters of your own existence. Ask

yourself "how am I?" you find there's nothing

there. The madman laughing in endless re-

cognition of God. Brave telescopes stroke

the stars. O little, bitter pill which art

in Heaven. I see through your mirrors in

the Big Glass Day, I see through your costumes

in the summer parade. The world of Stuff

and Things is not amenable to the

world of Transcendental Metaphysics.

These hands, these two, mute, useful tools, cannot

grip the water. We practise symmetry

on the supermarket shelves. We're ali-

ens looking for life on Mars, aliens

trying to make life in jars, aliens home-

sick for the stars, trying to find home in the

all-night bars. I've abjured nursing the suff-

ering of my ideals. Glow in the dark

stars on the ceiling fade. The blood-orange

dawn after a dark night of the soul is

more colourful and joyous than ever

before. I find this on ecstasy. Ec-

stasy got me talking to some strangers

at the lamp post called "Reality Check

Point" about the possibility of

injecting smack into the Univer-

sal Mind through the agency of snowfall.

Yes You May

I get my arm-wrestling strength from the void.

My energy comes from the void, that is.

Death, death clean as sugar. The fear of death

may be all that stops us being free. Dread

of dread and you're already dead. We need

catharsis by chaos; need to see dist-

ortion is clarity. Gnarled tree fingers

snap so easily. Nirvana buttons.

Nirvana pills. The mind all around you

on a slinky screen. Phew! What a cluttered up

mouthful! I am spitting teeth! Buddha knows

his cage bars are but the pyramidal

shafts of light when the sun is nearing the

horizon but behind a mountainous

cloud out to sea. Elephants have mourning

too. Sadness is an indulgent emo-

tion. Life is fragile. The forefront of myth-

ology is more physics and poet-

ry more about the mundane. The songs you

write reflect the colour and shape of your
guitar. O computer-face of psychic-
rash, the benign, smiling virus is spread-
ing. That travelling bit of mess that goes

with the clock. That party-crawl of senses,
crawling home, puking, apologising
profusely to inward grace. "Go to waste,"
was the command, from the end of a branch.
There's a hole in my arm where the rain gets
in. Stop fobbing me off with your compli-
ments, man. If the England captain can't un-
derstand something it's not likely to be
genius. The plane exists on 2 dimensions including Time. The pyramid

exists on 4 dimensions including
Time. But to turn a plane into a pyramid is a 1 dimensional step.
The spies are out but the spiral's in. Love
is a search for much small proof. I wish I

Yes You May

was away with the cloud-change, I wish I

was away with the starbeams, I wish I

was away with the mothership, I wish

I was away with the fairies. My feet

are in the clouds, I've got oxygen. Im-

agine if we changed all the 'ands' in the

world to 'buts'. If you reverse what they say

on the News you get nearer the truth. The

Lock Up where we record on binaural

earphones in Cambridge is a giant brain.

We're barefoot on the beach in days that have

lost their names. I listen until your words

are a warm, forgetful rain. I am strong-

er than heroin. A grain of smack in

the Sahara. A statue of Kate crumb-

ling in the centre of town. Under Ant-

arctica, black moon, fire sky. I don't

have heroes I only have friends. O cross-

roads of all inward spiral I hope your

mind does not go viral. Co-imagin-

ation is the key. Is-ness has been coined

before but not co-imaginative

vision. An orange dramatically

increases in is-ness after but half

an hour of meditation. So does a

glass of water. If I woke inside a

novel I'd kick a full stop down the street.

I'd crash my face into water at dawn.

No more would my consciousness be knocked back

at a remove from itself. The brain is

not a computer for it can self-heal.

I love you because you have ten senses.

I love you because you have ten senses.

I am but an invisible conduct-

or behind the words, the two-way mirror.

FOR THE FLEE

With Personism I address you,

and still wish to undress you

with secateurs preferably,

now the fretboard is a sea,

e' en though it's too late,

for hot cabbage on a plate.

This bubble, this apostrophe,

enrichened by catastrophe,

it pops and leaves the day

exhumed from wet clay.

I can only hope to deduce

that it is time for juice.

I am happy with the App

that fell down into my lap.

Such darkness as cast aside

by the roving of this tide

stinks a bit of the stench of black

owning less than a lack.

O you only turn me down

like the frowning of a clown.

Mother shoves it in the AGA,

at the end of this saga.

John Tucker

THE POLLEN'D DISTRACTIONARY

I invented the word distractionary

to contain such neologisms

as comnambulism, meaning

online sleepwalking, as

funger meaning hunger for fun,

as filence meaning delicate speech,

as amazeballs to replace archaic 'gay,'

as emocracy, meaning rule by emotion,

as agovernment, meaning

the opposite of government,

as gravitolution and evity

which might go without saying,

as co-imagination, as in to be

diagonalised by omnijective

interface of random access

co-imagination, which is not fun,

and I thought isness was another one,

as in music is penetration of isness,

but it was already done in Joyce,

whom it seems knew a lot of these,

and I have just thought of another,

not just "indwellable" meaning

the opposite of indomitable,

when it comes to cinema,

but the word entropy spelled backwards,

as if to frame the first, unformulated

spark of appetence in Nothingness, preceding

Creation, yet again, even though

the   universe   was   born   in   silence
not appetence as far as we know.

www.ingramcontent.com/pod-product-compliance
Lightning Source LLC
Chambersburg PA
CBHW031149160426
43193CB00008B/304